5.95

WHY A CHRISTIAN LEADER MAY FALL

Dr. Clyde M. Narramore

CROSSWAY BOOKS • WESTCHESTER, ILLINOIS
A DIVISION OF GOOD NEWS PUBLISHERS

Cover photography: William Koechling

Book design: K. L. Mulder

First printing, 1988

Printed in the United States of America

Library of Congress Catalog Card Number 88-71216

ISBN 0-89107-504-6

Contents

A Personal Word

One evening when my wife and I were leaving a store, a lady who recognized us walked up and greeted us. Then she said, "You are interested in religious things, aren't you?"

I agreed that we were, and I asked her about her spiritual interests.

"Well," she said, "I'm not into religion very much as yet, but I suppose as we get older it's natural to think about such things more. But I'm a little confused. For example, I've been watching television about some scandals that religious leaders have had." Then after a pause she asked, "What would cause strongly religious people to do such questionable things?"

When I asked her what she thought, she surprised me.

"Don't you think," she said in a compassionate tone, "that maybe they have some problems that are not religious in nature? Maybe they've fallen into trouble because they have some other kind of problem—maybe psychological."

As we finished our brief conversation I thought to myself, "I wish everyone had as much insight as this lady." Many people are wringing their hands wondering how religious leaders who are so strongly against sin can be living in sin.

And that's what I'd like to share with you in this book. I'd like to consider some of the major reasons why a Christian leader may fall. After all, unless we come to understand the real causes, we'll not be able to help leaders who have such problems. Nor will we know how to prevent similar tragedies in the lives of the young people who are growing up today and will become the Christian leaders of tomorrow.

Introduction

I t's an old story—very old. I first heard about it
when I was a boy about five or six years old.
I was raised on a ranch in a community where
we probably had no more than sixty or seventy people. There was just one church in the community, a
tiny church where the pastor preached the gospel and
won people to the Lord Jesus Christ.

I suppose my attitude toward the pastor was
about the same as everyone else's. He was looked up to
and respected. No, he wasn't a strong ranch hand like
most of the men in the community, but he didn't need
to be. He did his own thing—he preached Sunday
morning and night, and led a Bible study for the few
and faithful who came on Wednesday evening.

I remember hearing him preach about sin and salvation—about Heaven and Hell. He encouraged people to be saved.

Then one day I heard some grown-ups talking. They said something about the pastor leaving and not coming back. They said he had left his wife and had run away with a much younger woman. That was the kind of talk that circulated around the ranch houses and barns, and as far as I knew, it was true.

That was my first initiation to the problem of Christian leaders falling and living in sin.

But the problem is much older than that. In the Bible we read about a very great man, King David. He was a hero, a slayer of the giant, a man strong in battle, and the sweet-singer psalmist of Israel. He was married to the king's daughter and probably had a number of sex partners in the person of concubines. The Bible says this:

> Now it came to pass in the spring of the year, at the time when kings go out to battle, that David sent Joab and his servants with him, and all Israel; and they destroyed the people of Ammon and besieged Rabbah. But David stayed at Jerusalem. Then it happened one evening that David arose from his bed and walked on the roof of the king's house. And from the roof he saw a woman bathing, and the woman was very beautiful to behold. . . . So David sent

messengers, and took her; and she came to him,
and he lay with her. . . . And the woman
conceived and said . . . I am with child.
(2 Samuel 11:1-5)

You remember more of the story. David had done
this sinful thing with Bathsheba during the time that
her husband, Uriah, was away in the army, fighting a
battle. Before long, David sent for Uriah and asked
him to go to his home where he could be with his
wife. This, of course, was a manipulative effort on
David's part to make it appear that the child whom
Bathsheba had conceived was Uriah's own child. But
that didn't work. So David arranged to have Uriah
killed.

Not a pretty picture of a king, a popular leader,
and "a man after God's own heart."

Today in the twentieth century we see much the
same thing going on. Being a pioneer Christian psychologist and knowing many Christian leaders around
the world, I have seen some unbelievable situations
firsthand. Some of my greatest joys through the years
have been to associate with these fine and gifted men
of God. But on the other hand, one of my greatest
disappointments has been to know the intimate facts
about some Christian leaders who have fallen into sin
and have destroyed their ministries and the lives of
others.

The details and outcomes of these incidents have been unbelievably sordid and tragic, involving people, animals and objects. It would be difficult to conjure up in your mind the gross and sinful facts of the cases.

But does God continue to work His purposes in the midst of these scandals? Yes. God has a great and eternal plan for mankind and for each person on earth. So despite human sinfulness, and even in the midst of it, God works out His glorious redemptive intentions in the lives of those who look to Him and trust Him.

I know these things firsthand. I mentioned earlier that one of my first recollections was of the fall and immoral behavior of our beloved pastor. After he deserted his wife and ran away with a girl, God continued to work in our community.

The few families there continued to worship each Sunday. Our little country church was heated by a wood-burning stove that stood near the middle of the room on one side. We didn't need the stove most of the year, but we never got around to taking it out. So it was always there, with its black stovepipe extending up through the roof.

At the age of five or six I began to understand the gospel of Jesus Christ. The minister would talk about Heaven. But I didn't like that subject because I had made no preparations to go there. I also disliked his preaching about Hell because I had done nothing to sidestep that either. In fact, I was uncomfortable and against nearly everything he talked about. Before long I devised a little plan of my own. I would often sit on the bench, back of the stovepipe, so that the minister would not see me. I felt that if he wasn't looking me in the face, his message wouldn't bother me so much. So I was careful to always keep the stovepipe between myself and the preacher.

Young as I was, God's Holy Spirit was seeking an entrance into my life, but I was refusing to yield to Him. And the stovepipe was my ally.

The Bible says there are three kinds of "stovepipes":

(1) the lust of the flesh,
(2) the lust of the eye,
(3) the pride of life.

The Word of God teaches that all sin can be fitted into those three categories. These, of course, are the very things that keep people from trusting Christ as their Savior. So for a number of years, whenever I attended church I tried to sit back of the stovepipe.

Finally one day, riding a horse, driving some cattle into a corral, I thought about the fact that it was time for me to get out from behind the stovepipe. So that very day when I got the cattle in the corral, I closed the gate, threw the reins over the head of the horse, and tied him to a post nearby. Then I went over by a ditch bank just a few steps away and knelt down and prayed something like this: "God, I believe You made Heaven and earth and You made me. Therefore I'm responsible to You. I know I'm a sinner, and I believe that Your Son, Jesus Christ, died for sinners like me. I want You to come into my heart just now and forgive me of my sins. And I will serve You as long as I live. Amen."

I got up from my knees, and I knew I was marvelously saved. I had signed the contract.

"For whoever calls upon the name of the Lord shall be saved." I called on Him—therefore I knew I was saved. Romans 10:13 had become a reality in my heart regardless of the immoral garbage that had been putrifying in the parsonage.

The next day, playing ball at school, everything was different. Going through college, things were different. Now working professionally around the world, everything is different: all because of the relationship with God which was established that day on the ranch.

What happens when this right relationship with God is established—when a man accepts Christ as his Savior?

God's Holy Spirit indwells your life and brings some immediate changes which can never be explained outside of the fact that God has performed a miracle. But this is not all. The Holy Spirit ministers to that person through the years. Consequently, he has the potential for changing as he reads God's Word and obeys it, developing qualities which a person can never bring about by his own volition. They are gifts of God that can never be "psyched up."

While God was working in my heart, and changing my life, He was doing the same in the lives of millions of others around the world . . . regardless of the behavior of some Christian leaders!

1
Shocked by the News

Although the public
is shocked by immorality
on the part of a prominent leader,
God isn't.

And there is
no creature hidden from His sight,
but all things are naked
and open to the eyes of Him
to whom we must give account.
Hebrews 4:13

When you and I suddenly hear about a Christian leader who has fallen into sin, we are shocked. At first we can't believe it. Or we refuse to believe it. We don't want it to be true, so we try to deny it.

In years past denial was easier than it is today. Before the time we had television we may have heard about a scandal. But if it was far away from us, we probably never knew for sure if it was true, so we could easily deny it. But today it's different. As soon as a Christian leader falls, news reporters, like thirsty bloodhounds, descend upon the guilty one and do almost everything except exact his blood. This is especially true of news-gatherers who are unsaved and who feel that sinful tragedies of Christian leaders are not only juicy headliners, but also a devastating slap in the face to Christianity, which they may dislike anyway.

But this shouldn't surprise any believer who knows God's Word. The Bible clearly teaches that the unsaved person, as bright or well-educated as he may be, cannot possibly understand spiritual things. "But the natural man does not receive the things of the Spirit of God, for they are foolishness to him; nor can he know them because they are spiritually discerned" (1 Corinthians 2:14).

One of the great facts of spiritual conversion is the entrance of God's Holy Spirit into the very being of the person who is genuinely saved. The Holy Spirit indwelling and working in the believer's life, and opening the Scriptures, gives him godly wisdom which is unknown to those who are unsaved. This truth is underscored in 1 Corinthians 1:18—"For the message of the cross is foolishness to those who are perishing, but to us who are being saved it is the power of God."

So we cannot expect unsaved reporters, newsmen and commentators to understand or appreciate spiritual things. They may be clever and well-informed in some areas, yet have no comprehension of Biblical matters.

If money, high living, gold-plated Cadillacs, and other indulgent practices are part of the story, reporters lap it up. They think their "firsthand" story will really stir people emotionally. It's amazing how some unsaved people will tolerate at least a measure of immorality, while on the other hand they get absolutely choked up regarding money matters. Undoubtedly, the reason for this twisted perception is because most of them know deep in their hearts that they have committed many sins themselves. So a Christian leader's moral downfall makes the average unsaved person feel less guilty. But since he may never have had an opportunity to make a great deal of money and live "high on the hog," he resents it deeply. And since he is not tithing himself or giving his money to the Lord's work, he justifies his own greed by poking fun at "poor stupid Christians" who give their hard-earned money to their church or to another Christian ministry.

Although the public is shocked by immorality on the part of a prominent leader, God isn't. Nor is the offender. Serious problems have long root systems. They go back for many years. Problems don't just happen; they usually start small in one's early years, then grow and grow. The offender may have struggled with a problem for decades. Then finally he is found out. People sit at their TVs stunned by what they hear or see. But, of course, they have no idea how long the problem has been going on, and how it has developed.

Such was the case of "Steve" (not his real name), who was in full-time Christian service. He was middle-aged, the father of several children, and a respected leader among his people. He was known for his strong spiritual commitment, his motto being "Set for the Defense of the Gospel."

His followers were admonished to avoid worldliness in all of its forms. He had little to do with other Christian leaders because, as he said, "They're compromisers, and the Bible teaches us to not be unequally yoked with unbelievers."

People coming into his congregation were thoroughly quizzed about their complete allegiance to God and His Word. Not only did he screen his people carefully, he preached separation loud and clear. His Bible messages were punctuated by strong condemnations of other religious groups and false teachings. He checked everyone to see that he or she was using the right version of the Bible.

He set unusually high standards for his own family. He continually told his wife that she really knew very little about theology and that she would have to spend more time in study so she could attain a higher level of spirituality. In a sense she respected his high standards of Christian living, but she felt she would never be able to "catch up with him."

The children were kept in a subservient role, then sent away to a Christian school as early as possible. They thought of their father as a spiritual giant to whom they could probably never measure up. His word was law, and that was that. His ways with his followers were autocratic and final and based, as he said, on "Biblical principles."

If his people had taken a peek behind the psychological curtain, they might have put two and two together. Although his actions were bathed and clothed in "deep spirituality," a careful observer would have noted that his personality was marked by a high level of anger and criticism. They would have seen that he regularly distanced himself from his children, his wife, his followers, and other Christian leaders. In addition, a careful observer would have noticed that he would tolerate only those close assistants who never questioned his point of view. But no one looked behind the psychological curtain. Those who liked him stayed with him. Those who didn't went elsewhere. Consequently a selective process was taking place through the years. Those who liked him, or who were *like* him, remained, forming a group of like-minded people.

But finally, after many years, the bubble burst. This Christian leader was apprehended for child molestation and sexual abuse! The court required that he have psychiatric evaluation. During those sessions it was learned that he had been committing such crimes for years. In fact his adolescent years were marked by turmoil and confusion. As a young child he had been molested by an older boy and an uncle. He had never received help for his problems, so his strong "spiritual stand" had become a defense against his own sinful behavior.

One should not conclude that a strong spiritual emphasis is usually a defense against one's true feelings. It is not. But when a person considers a whole pattern of behavior, it may point to possible basic maladjustments.

How long had this man's problems persisted? Nearly all his life. And this is true of most severe problems; they have long root systems. Although we may be shocked by the news of a person falling into sin, we can usually be assured that the problem has existed in some form for many years.

This also gives us some concept of how long it may take to resolve a long-time, severe problem. There is no magic wand we can wave and say, "Be gone, at once, forever!"

2
Rank and Its Privileges

People often
extend privileges to leaders
who unfortunately capitalize
on them.

> For you, brethren,
> have been called to liberty;
> only do not use liberty
> as an opportunity for the flesh,
> but through love serve one another.
> *Galatians 5:13*

We've all heard the saying, "Rank has its privileges." This carries with it the thought that a person who is in a high position, one who holds a special office, or one who has unusual talent and influence also has the right to do whatever he chooses. I suppose that all of us who are in positions of leadership have overstepped our bounds in some way. We may expect special attention or favors because of "Who We Are." Society also seems to go along with this. Institutions and organizations are tuned in to recognizing certain people because of their influence or position.

Several years ago I traveled with a well-known man for several days. As soon as his name appeared on the airline passengers list, a representative of that airline was assigned to get him on the plane before others and to extend several favors. Since he and I were traveling companions I saw this special treatment firsthand. My friend, the star, certainly did not ask for special attention. The company extended it to him quite naturally. My point is this: not only do some people expect special attention, the society in which we live naturally accords it. So it is easy for a person in a leadership role to become accustomed to feeling that because he is afforded privileges, he actually deserves them. And it's only a short step from feeling you deserve them to demanding them. This has been innate in the downfall of many leaders.

For example, I was riding one day with a prominent local man on a brand-new superhighway. When we reached the end of this big, beautiful road, we saw an official warning sign that said we would have to take a detour. But the man who was driving the car said, "We don't have to take a detour. Another ten miles of this new highway has been completed, and I'm going to move these barriers and go straight ahead."

So he did. Then he got back in the car, stepped on the gas, and away we went down this big new stretch of road which was not yet open to the public. After a few miles, we heard a police siren coming up close behind us and signaling us to stop. My friend, the driver, slammed on the brakes, jumped out of the car, and dashed over to the highway patrolman as though he was going to attack him. In fact, he did attack him with words. "What's the matter with you," he asked the policeman, "don't you know who I am? Well, let me tell you. I have a right to use this road if I want to and no one is going to stop me, and if you try to make trouble for me, I'll report you. The chief of police is my closest friend. Here, take my card and go peddle your papers."

My driver evidently believed that since he was a big shot in town, came from a prominent family, and had plenty of dollars in the bank, he had every right to pull his rank and enjoy certain privileges that other men didn't have.

Occasionally Christian leaders may have some of these feelings and not really be aware of it. Their "positions" tend to extend liberties that they "capitalize" on. David, in the Bible, evidently felt this same way. He wanted what he wanted when he wanted it, and no one could stop him.

A Christian leader often has the resources to do what he wishes. He usually has staff and people around him to carry out his purposes. In addition, he may also have the authority to do what he wishes. Take David, in the Bible, for example.

In the book of 2 Samuel, chapter 11, we see

that many of these factors were true of David. It was spring of the year when kings were going out to battle. But since David was in charge he decided not to go. He had that authority.

Since David was in charge and had a large organization, he selected Joab to go. David also cleared out Joab's servants from his house and sent them to battle too. In other words, David had the authority, the financial resources, and the personnel to do what he wished.

The Bible does not tell us so, but we can well imagine that David had the whole scenario well in mind weeks before he took Bathsheba.

The Bible goes on to say that one evening David arose from his bed and walked out on the roof of the king's house. He could do this because he was in charge and no one would question him.

Then David sent messengers over to Bathsheba, who had been bathing, and they brought her to David. The average person could not have done this. But again, David had the authority and the personnel to pull off the whole sinful act.

As you read the rest of the story of David trying to cover his sin and eventually having Bathsheba's husband killed, you can see that he was able to do it because of his authority, his personnel, and his money.

Sometimes even a Christian leader who is supposed to be a humble example to others uses his rank and privileges to take advantage of other people and to commit immoral acts.

Unfortunately, when a well-known Christian leader falls into sin, believers who are close to the situation often make a much greater effort to reinstate him rather than to help the victim.

Some time ago a trusted Christian leader had a series of sexual affairs with a young lady in the community. As the months went by, people did almost everything possible to understand him, to talk to him, and to reinstate him in Christian service. But they seemed to forget the girl whom he had violated and ruined. She was left on her own to abort or deliver the baby. When someone asked why the local leaders had taken so much time with the offender and had done virtually nothing to help the girl, one person said, "Oh . . . I guess we didn't think about her!"

This erroneous mind-set affects some Christian leaders when it comes to many things, including sex. They have been deluded into thinking that they can do whatever they wish with their wives, people in the church, various women, and others. Instead of being called to be servants, they feel that "the territory" allows special privileges. They disregard the Scriptures that warn: "You have been called to liberty; only do not use liberty as an opportunity for the flesh, but by love serve one another" (Galatians 5:13). And, "All of you be subject one to another, and be clothed with humility; for God resists the proud, but gives grace to the humble" (1 Peter 5:5).

There are some Christian leaders who are more vulnerable to immorality than others. Although such leaders emphasize God's Word, their ministry is really not very sound or dependable. In fact, they have some of the same personality characteristics that religious cult leaders have.

Not all leaders of cults are alike by any means. They have different backgrounds, personality dynamics, and motivations. Nevertheless, certain traits tend to mark these leaders who draw people to them and win amazing, almost blind loyalty.

(1) They are often dynamic, forceful personalities with unusual persuasive powers. People are captivated by these qualities and are oblivious to the strong leader's brainwashing techniques. They don't recognize problems in their leader, and frequently look no further before linking up with his good-sounding cause.

(2) The leader is usually poorly adjusted. At first he may seem competent—having it all together. In fact, he may give the impression that he is very outstanding. But if you were to know him personally, you would discover that he has many deep psychological problems. For example, he may be hostile

or basically insecure. He may be paranoid and unable to trust others as he should. His personality deficits may lead him to establish a cult and persevere in its development. In this way he can work around his hang-ups. He's free to act any way he wishes without losing his job or being criticized by those around him.

(3) These leaders are often self-appointed and generally self-perpetuating. Since no one has appointed them, no one can throw them out. They may have a board whom they dominate. Sometimes there is no board to control or govern the leader. He is a law unto himself.

(4) Frequently the leader is very bright, a highly intelligent individual. He is able to develop clever plans and programs. He is also likely to abound in energy. He goes and goes, and seldom slows down.

(5) The cult leader usually sees his ministry as the only significant one in all the world. He is dedicated 110 percent to what he is doing, to the exclusion of all others. He is so captivated by his own ministry that he persuades his followers to disregard other ministries. In fact, he may train his people to shield themselves from any and all other teachings; and amazingly, his followers usually do so. In other words they are not only completely loyal to the cult ministry, but they are also aggressively against all other religious groups.

Although a Christian leader who is heading for a downfall may be talented with unusual skills, he may have serious personality hang-ups. Like the cult leader, the three or so types of personality problems which he is likely to have are (1) hostility, (2) insecurity, and (3) paranoia.

An angry, critical spirit may pop out in the most unexpected ways. Deep insecurity may cause him to work overtime to be successful. His paranoia may show itself in not trusting people or other organizations. He may talk against them. He may gather a few devoted and like-minded people around him and work with them the best he can. But he does not fully trust most people. And, in fact, he may not trust his closest friends. He keeps an emotional distance. But because of his rank he takes many privileges, like David in the Bible. Then he falls and brings disgrace upon the cause of Christ.

The secular world may not have very high ethical standards. Sometimes almost anything goes. I was talking with a missionary one day as I was working with a group of Christian leaders overseas. "One of the problems we have here," he said, "is the intimidation that our Christian young ladies experience when they begin working in the offices of governmental officials or businessmen. When a lady takes a job it is understood that she will automatically become the boss's sex partner."

Unfortunately, there are a few so-called Christian men who likewise feel that all they administer is theirs personally, or that they are entitled to what they want.

3
Public
Vulnerability

There's a
price to be paid
for being continually
in the public's eye.

A man's gift
makes room for him,
and brings him before great men.
Proverbs 18:16

A show which has projected itself on the American TV screen during the past few years highlights the lives of the rich and famous. The host rambles on and on about luxury living. He may show, for example, a Pacific paradise with coconut palms gently kissed by tropical breezes, and crystal waters reflecting the perpetual sunshine of this sensuous hideaway.

But there's another side of this idyllic haven. Little is said about the public exposure and vulnerability of these famous people whose names and faces are recognized by even the most humble. In a sense, they are like prisoners in their own homes. For example, a man said recently that he dared not go out of his house for five days after something had been said about him on national TV. "The photographers and reporters were hiding in the bushes all around the house and behind nearly every tree," he said. "They were stalking me, getting ready to get the scoop just as soon as I walked out the front or back door, or crawled out of a side window."

Most people would probably give anything to be either rich or famous. But there's a price to be paid for being continually in the public's eye. And this price is sometimes paid by a well-known Christian leader.

There are certain disturbed people who walk the streets, sit in church pews, and listen to the radio. At first glance they seem normal. But these same people have unbelievable problems. They may dress like the rest of us, but they think quite differently. These maladjusted people may, for example, see sexual possibilities in a leader that a leader doesn't even see in himself! I talked with a woman once, for instance, who fell in love long-distance with a radio preacher. "Oh," she told me, "his voice is so rich and beautiful—he really turns me on."

In another instance, the chairman of a deacons' board phoned me asking what they should do about a lady in their church who had a fixation on the pastor. She spent much of her time thinking of how handsome he was when he stood in the pulpit and read the Scriptures. One day she confided to a friend, "If I can't have him, I'll kill him because I couldn't bear to think of anybody else having him."

Such disturbed people are coming out of the woodwork more and more these days. They will follow a prominent person around the country just to look at and touch him. Their fantasies are lucid and lurid. What is worse, they conjure up a host of uncanny methods of trapping him anywhere they can—church, hotel, beach, or elsewhere.

Not just a few leaders have either knowingly or unwittingly been ruined by such women. The average Christian who goes about his daily work serving the Lord may never realize all the traps that Satan is able to set for the leader who is publicly vulnerable.

A serious problem may arise when one of these disturbed women begins to have close contacts (perhaps in counseling sessions) with a pastor or some other Christian leader who also has unresolved problems.

Not long ago, for example, a minister asked me how to keep women from falling in love with him. "When I counsel with a woman," he said, "she may likely want to have an affair with me."

"That's interesting," I said. "I've never had that problem, but I'm not handsome . . . But neither are you! You are wanting women to fall in love with you. You have severe problems yourself, and you give them many small signals to have an affair with you."

Such was the case of a woman, presumably a Christian, who was strongly attracted to her pastor. He was an outgoing man, rather outwardly affectionate. He thought nothing of "sweet-talking" his lady church members and occasionally putting his arm around one and saying, "You know the Lord loves you—and so do I."

This particular woman, who was lonely and unstable, responded to his "caring attitude." She saw real possibilities in him. She often fantasized about him. She could see them together in many situations. She had been raised in a family where she was starved for affection. She learned early in childhood that she would have to manipulate people if she were to survive. So she did—and in time she became skilled in the art of manipulation.

She managed to have several counseling sessions with the pastor. She sensed that he would respond favorably to her overtures because of his reactions during the personal counseling sessions. Little by little she built him up by telling him how helpful he was. "I would give anything," she would say, "if my husband was like you—so intelligent and loving and kind."

The pastor, like many counselors, was enjoyably flattered during his sessions with her. In time she shared more personal problems about her husband. Little by little she shared how sexually inadequate her husband was.

The pastor's own sex life was far from desirable. Down deep he longed for a warm, loving wife with whom he could have fulfilling intimate relations. Both were emotionally immature and vulnerable. In time they were meeting secretly and committing adultery.

The Bible teaches, "Be sure your sins will find you out." And so they did. The pastor resigned, moved to another state and began a new "ministry," never getting the professional help he so desperately needed. The dynamics at work in his personality structure were still there, and would continue to persist for years to come.

These same Christian leaders may not be having such experiences if they were not in the public eye, meeting people day after day, and having continued, personal contacts with them.

4
Pride Goeth Before

A leader may
cut out relationships and resources
by which he can measure humility,
reality and accountability.

Pride
goeth before destruction,
and a haughty spirit
before a fall.
Proverbs 16:18

One of the most insightful verses in the Bible is Proverbs 16:18. It is often quoted when a person has fallen or sinned or destroyed himself: "Pride goeth before destruction, and a haughty spirit before a fall."

It suggests that a person's downfall is likely to be of his own doing. Pride as used in the above verse carries with it the thought of lifting up and exalting oneself. In a sense pride is a wall-building exercise. A man may turn to himself to such an extent that he locks others out.

A person may come to trust so much in himself that he doesn't need the advice or scrutiny of other people. In an unwarranted sense of his own superiority he essentially says, "I can do it myself." Such a person has an inordinate self-importance attitude.

The picture which we find in Proverbs 16:18 is a fortress raised up to maintain and contain a malignant self-indulgence. In essence, the wall which a Christian leader may unknowingly erect cuts out relationships and resources by which we measure humility, reality and accountability.

And that's dangerous.

Each of us needs those around us who can wisely advise us and point out things about ourselves or our procedures which are not sound. If we don't have such safeguards, we are likely to think that the real world around us is what we "think" it is, rather than what it really is.

Christian leaders sometimes have such problems. It may develop in part because of their talents. Nearly all leaders, and especially Christian leaders, are truly gifted. And they're gifted all over. Many have had to choose their vocation from among several. They could have been successful in music, athletics, medicine, law, politics, education and other professions. And as God's Word says, "A man's gift makes room for him, and brings him before great men" (Proverbs 18:16). In other words, his talents bring him to the attention of people.

When a leader is highly gifted, he may tend to rely on his talents, almost to the exclusion of depending upon God. In time he may pray less and trust less, but depend more and more on his own unusual abilities. This is often the beginning of pride. "I can do it myself . . . I can figure out my own ways . . . I don't need others . . . I can develop my own plans and make them work . . . Just stand by and let me do my own thing . . . I can think . . . I have talent . . . I can make things go by myself."

But such thinking is contrary to God's Word: "Every good gift and every perfect gift is from above, and comes down from the Father of lights, with whom there is no variation or shadow of turning" (James 1:17).

Every talent we have is given to us by God, and it should be used for His glory. Taking credit for our talent is in direct opposition to Biblical truth: "And what hast thou that thou didst not receive? Now if thou didst receive it, why dost thou glory, as if thou hadst not received it?" (1 Corinthians 4:7).

On the other hand, it is easy to think that a Christian leader is prideful when actually he's not. The average person may look at a leader and say to himself, "He thinks he's a big shot." But such a statement may tell you more about the insecurity and low self-image of the accuser than it does about the Christian leader.

Men and women who are in positions of leadership are usually bright, dynamic, forceful, visionary, multitalented, and skillful. These God-given talents may combine to cause a person to be somewhat separated from those around him and to do things differently. But it does not mean, necessarily, that he has a problem with pride.

However, not a few men have fallen because they were caught up in themselves. They were prideful, and they planted their own seeds of destruction.

5
What's at Home?

A man's ideas,
his performance, his actions
reflect his home life.

An excellent wife
is the crown of her husband,
but she who causes shame is
like rottenness in his bones.
Proverbs 12:4

Through the years I've noticed that a man always brings his wife to work with him. In a sense he never comes alone. A man's ideas, his performance, his actions reflect his home life. If he's happy at home and things are going well, you will notice it during the day when he's on the job.

But if, on the other hand, a man is quarreling with his wife, or they are in serious disagreement, or if there are problems with the children . . . these will show up eventually in his daily performance. This is especially true of pastors, evangelists, and other Christian leaders since they are speaking and ministering to numbers of people. Their preaching or other actions will reflect either happiness or unhappiness at home.

I wish it were possible for all men and women in Christian leadership positions to be happily married and fulfilled with their families. But such is not always the case.

In fact, some men travel a great deal and hold meetings from state to state partially in an effort to get away from their wives and from an unpleasant situation at home.

For example, a Christian leader said to me, "I am afforded a measure of respect everywhere except at home. When I'm out preaching or speaking at a conference, people respect me. But the minute I walk inside the door in my own home, I'm yelled at, criticized, nagged, and put down. And it has been this way for nearly all of our married life. I came from a peaceful home where there was a great deal of love. And when I married I thought my wife and I would have much the same kind of home. But I soon learned differently. Even on our honeymoon, my wife had a tantrum, picked up a vase from the dresser in the hotel, and threw it at me. She barely missed my head as she broke the window. I looked up, completely shocked, and asked her what was wrong. She walked the other way and said, 'You'll never know.' "

This Christian leader went on to tell me that,

indeed, he didn't know what the problem was and that in twenty-five years of marriage he still doesn't know.

A Christian leader who operates from such an unhappy home platform is vulnerable to a woman who comes along and shows him special love and affection. Literally hundreds of pastors, evangelists, and other Christian leaders have been tempted by immorality because there was little, if any, love coming their way from their own spouse.

Of course, the fault is not always on one side. The wife may be the well-adjusted one who year after year has to put up with a critical, unloving husband who is not well-adjusted and who is more interested in his work than he is in his home.

What makes it worse is that a Christian leader may find it difficult to admit to an unhappy marriage, too ashamed to admit that his home and marriage are in shambles. After preaching to and helping others, he may think it is almost impossible to go for help himself.

At one time I was counseling with an evangelist's wife who blatantly said, "My husband doesn't have any grounds for divorce. I have never been unfaithful to him even one time. According to the Bible, he can't get a divorce."

But when I asked her if his accusation was true—that they had not had intimate relations with each other in seven years—she said, "That's true, but what has that got to do with his getting a divorce? I just don't like sex."

If you were to study cases of immorality among Christian leaders, you would find that many of them do not gain much satisfaction at home. This does not justify their sinful actions, but it does help to understand why some leaders have engaged in immorality.

6
Emotional Adjustment

When our lives
are marked by childhood
emotional deprivations,
we will go to almost any extent
and engage in bizarre behavior
in an effort to meet those needs.

Blessed is the man
to whom the Lord does not impute iniquity
and in whose spirit there is no guile.
Psalm 32:2

As a child is growing up, he has basic emotional needs. These needs are put in the heart of each infant by God Himself. This is the way He has designed and made us. You and I are not only physical beings—we are also spiritual beings and emotional beings.

It's the responsibility of mothers and fathers to meet the basic emotional needs of their children from the time they are born until they are grown. These emotional needs include feeling you are loved, knowing you are worthwhile, feeling that you belong, being relatively free from fear, and feeling relatively free from guilt. Families should be living in such a way that the emotional needs are being met day by day.

But in many homes—perhaps most homes—parents may not be aware of these emotional needs, much less meeting them. Mothers and dads may have their own concerns, so they can't get around to meeting the emotional needs of their children. For example, a father may feel negative, angry and hostile because of the way he was treated during the years of his childhood. Such a father may find it almost impossible to forget his own feelings of resentment and reach out and show affection to his sons or daughters. Sometimes a family has been seriously broken so that a child goes through a divorce and feels the ravages of it even more than his parents.

Some parents are unhappy with each other. For example, women have often said to me such things as, "Trying to live with my husband is like walking on light bulbs. You never know when he's going to blow up or put me down about something."

Such parents are struggling with their own difficulties and are not in a position to reach out and meet the emotional needs of their sons and daughters.

In time the child becomes a teenager and finally an adult with negative, unhealthy feelings about himself. And the same glasses which we use to look at ourselves are those which we use to look at other people. Thus, if we have unhappy feelings about ourselves, we will have a measure of distortion as we perceive others. We may be jealous or envious, or we may be angry at them, or we may "worship" them, or run away from them, or continually seek their favor. These personality traits show up clearly on personality and psychological tests.

A person may go along in life and not really be aware of his emotional deprivations which stem from childhood. But they are there just the same, preventing him from having desirable feelings about himself.

For example, a Christian leader may have many negative feelings. He may feel he's not as good as others. To compensate, he may throw himself into his ministry with great force, never realizing he is trying to do things that will make him feel good about himself. He wants a bigger ministry, a larger house, more automobiles, and a host of other things. In other words, he is trying to get a higher position in a world of things to make up for his own low self-image.

But, of course, things and position never meet the need in his heart. Nevertheless, he tries to get more and to identify with significant people.

A Christian? Yes, he loves the Lord and he has many fine qualities, but he is vulnerable to many sinful things that might come his way. For example, a woman may entice him and build him up. He may feel that it's important for him to "conquer" this woman and have an affair with her.

No one resolves his problems, however, by entering into a sinful relationship; this only makes matters worse. Finally, the truth of his actions comes to light, and people are shocked and surprised. But a professionally trained person who had been observing this man could have predicted that it would undoubtedly happen sooner or later. When our lives are marked by childhood emotional deprivation, we will go to almost any extent and engage in bizarre behavior in an effort to meet these needs.

Of the many people whom I have known through the years, this has been true. If a Christian leader is insecure or has other personality problems, he becomes a "sitting duck" for almost any sinful thing that comes his way.

Simply because a person dresses well, is bright, knowledgeable, talented, and directs a large organization and has a lot of things doesn't necessarily mean that he's in good shape emotionally. And his emotional lacks can be used by Satan to get him all tangled up in life!

It is difficult for you or me to be deeply spiritual if we have severe hang-ups. A closeness to the Lord is hard to attain if, for example, we are paranoid and suspicious, not being able to trust others— or the Lord. Or, on the other hand, if we have a deep-seated insecurity (of which we may not even be aware) it may get in the way of feeling secure around fellow-Christians, or with Christ Himself.

I knew a pastor, for example, who was a gifted speaker. When he came to the Narramore Christian Foundation for two weeks of training at our Seminar for Ministers and Missionaries, he was given several psychological tests. All of the tests showed that he was definitely hostile. It was second-nature for him to look at situations and criticize them. He could easily "set people straight." His messages contained numerous negative "insights." He was bright, and he gave his analytical comments freely. He often told his wife and children what to do. You seldom saw him laughing and asking other people (including his church and family) how they felt—and what their ideas were. But he didn't realize he was this way. (Seldom do any of us realize this.)

When he was confronted by the counselor at the seminar about his negative thinking and his hostility, he became angry. Later on, after getting help and working through his problem, he said, "When the psychologist pointed out my negative traits, I felt like punching him in the nose."

Needless to say, this pastor, with all of his Bible knowledge and his study of the Word, was barricaded by his hostility from a real depth of spirituality. It is difficult to be all we could be spiritually if our personality problems have never been detected and resolved.

It is understandable that leaders who have unresolved problems find it easy to fall away and commit immoral acts. They are prime candidates for Satan's sinful attacks.

If you could bring together a thousand men and women who are in positions of Christian leadership, you would find a variety of emotional adjustment among them. They would range all the way from well-adjusted to very poorly adjusted.

Some would be composed, others always nervous. Some would be cheerful, others usually depressed. Some would be optimistic, others persistently pessimistic. Some would be outgoing, others inhibited. Some would be sympathetic; others would have shallow feelings. Some would be objective, others nearly always subjective. Some would be flexible, others rigid. Some would be amiable, others characteristically negative and hostile. Some would be deliberate, others impulsive. Some would be energetic, others usually lethargic. Some would have good, healthy feelings about themselves; others would have a low self-image. Some would be respectful, others continually manipulative. Some would be open to people, others introverted. Some would be secure, others always insecure. Some would be helpful, others overly domineering. Some would have a great deal of personal insight, while others would be lacking in understanding their own dynamics.

An important factor is this: those who are not personally well-adjusted would be most likely to become entangled in moral problems. In an unconscious attempt to fulfill basic emotional needs, they would tend to be vulnerable to a whole variety of negative experiences and immoral acts.

7
Pre-salvation Experiences

The less emotional
and sexual garbage we bring into
adulthood, and into our new life in Christ,
the less opportunity it has to
raise its ugly head later on.

Flee also youthful lusts;
but pursue righteousness, faith, love, peace
with those who call on the Lord
out of a pure heart.
2 Timothy 2:22

Each experience that you and I have is significant. It's evidently stored away in our mental/emotional computer where it remains throughout life. When we have the same experience over and over, the impression in our computer seems to be imprinted more deeply than if it were only a one-time or an occasional occurrence.

Of course, there are some experiences which are traumatic. They are so strong or startling that they leave an indelible mark upon our lives. These traumas stem from a variety of experiences, including bodily harm and the violation of one's own moral principles. They may produce long-lasting guilt or fear or twisted behavior later on. An interesting fact about traumatic experiences, or even other experiences, is that they may linger in our subconscious, causing us to have certain feelings without our realizing that these dynamics are going on inside us.

Experiences of life, especially those that take place before we are born again—prior to the time we trust Christ as our personal Savior—are especially significant to Christians. They may influence a person years after he is saved and has become a Christian leader. For example, an unsaved person may have been raised around godless people and may have indulged in cursing and swearing. In fact, foul talking may have become his usual way of life. All of this was going into his mental/emotional computer and was stored away. But years later it may pop out when the right key is pushed.

I once counseled with a man who was a remarkably fine Bible teacher. One day he said to me, "I can't understand it. I love the Lord with all my heart, and I believe that God has given me ability to teach the Word of God. I also strive to live a holy life day by day. But occasionally when something goes wrong and I become frustrated or angry, I suddenly find myself swearing like you wouldn't believe. It seems to come without warning, and, of course, I'm terribly ashamed and repentant."

We talked about this, and he told me that when he was a young person, unsaved and living in the world, cursing, swearing and using vile language was a part of his daily experience. He told me that as a young man, before salvation, he would get angry about something and curse to the hilt. As we discussed the problem, he began to see the relationship of the strong, persistent patterns of his pre-salvation days and how they were undoubtedly affecting him occasionally now that he was older and teaching God's Word.

So it is with sexual experiences. Even as believers in Jesus Christ, certain conditions and happenings can trigger old patterns and tempt a person to unwholesome immoral conduct. This is especially true if a person has not had professional counseling and has not consciously dealt with it. Christian leaders who have had many immoral experiences before they were saved may find themselves reverting to these sinful patterns. And simply vowing that you will not do it again does not take care of the problem. The problem needs special attention. It is indeed important to be saved as early as possible and to live a consistent life for Christ. The less sexual garbage we bring into our new life in Christ, the less opportunity it has to raise its ugly head later on.

Not long ago I had the privilege of serving for more than a year on the Attorney General's Task Force on Family Violence. The committee was comprised of nine leaders, each representing a professional specialty. Since I was the only psychologist, I was expected to give special attention to psychological aspects of family violence and the treatment of victims.

For more than a year we traveled to various parts of the United States where we conducted hearings in major population areas. All sections of the nation, including Hawaii and Alaska, were represented.

Typically we would meet in a given city for two or three days. A committee of several attorneys and others from the Attorney General's office would prepare for the hearings. We would hear testimonies throughout the day from victims representing ten or twelve states. We also heard testimonies from researchers and from organizations that had desirable programs and facilities for rehabilitating victims.

The heart-rending testimonies were much the same from state to state. Perhaps two things stood out in the hearings: (1) the frequent use of alcohol in cases of home violence and (2) the frequency of sexual and emotional abuse in homes where violence was common.[1]

A study of Christian men and women who are

-----

[1]For a discussion of emotional and sexual abuse in childhood see the author's book *Parents at Their Best*.

having marriage and sex problems would reveal an inordinately high percentage who had been victims of sexual abuse in childhood. This type of abuse tends to follow a person throughout life, causing him or her to have personality and sex problems for years to come. Most sexual abuse victims do not share the information with anyone, causing a festering and smoldering of the problem which affects various areas of their lives.

Here are some of the more common problems caused by sexual abuse:

(1) A person is likely to develop a low self-image, feeling he or she is dirty and defiled, unworthy and unloved.

(2) One usually has guilt feelings that pervade many areas of living, and which prevent him from being at his best in life.

(3) He or she tends not to trust others, even close family members, including husband or wife.

(4) A person may develop twisted ideas about sex. These thoughts may take a whole host of forms in adulthood. These dynamics are rarely understood by the adult who has them.

(5) One may have little interest in sexual relations, even though he or she has a loving, understanding mate.

(6) One who has been sexually molested in childhood is quite likely to grow up with a tendency

to molest other children and young people as he or she was molested.

(7) A person who has been sexually abused in childhood may grow up to think of sex as a commodity or a weapon.

In summary, the pre-salvation experiences of people are very important in understanding and rehabilitating a person who is having problems of sex.

8
Psychosexual Development

Day by day,
and through many sources,
a child gradually develops feelings
and attitudes about his
and other people's sexuality.

And Jesus
increased in wisdom
and stature, and in favor
with God and men.
Luke 2:52

It is satisfying for a parent to watch his child grow through childhood. Little by little he or she grows taller and heavier. Features become pronounced. Adult characteristics begin to take shape.

But there is another type of development which is not so obvious. It is the child's psychosexual development. The term *psychosexual* has to do with mental and emotional attitudes which a person holds toward himself as a sexual being and toward other people as sexual beings. These attitudes are determined primarily by dynamics in the family, and without the conscious awareness of either the child or his parents. Of course, they can also be influenced by factors outside the home.

Day by day a child gradually develops feelings and attitudes about himself and his sexuality. As a boy lives with a well-adjusted father, he comes to appreciate the fact that Dad is a male and he himself also is a male. Good, positive feelings spring up from within him regarding his sexuality. At an emotional level he can say, "I like being a boy!" Correspondingly, he has healthy attitudes toward members of the opposite sex, because he is comfortable in his own sex role. Similarly, a boy who is raised by a well-adjusted mother develops good feelings about being a male. So the reinforcement comes from both parents.

In like manner, girls need well-adjusted mothers from whom they can absorb healthy feelings. Automatically, little girls are continuously picking up countless cues that Mom is sending out. Hopefully these cues transmitted by Mom are saying, "I like being a woman!" If Mom is truly happy about being a woman, and happy about her husband, and respects him, the daughter will likely experience happy feelings about being a girl. If Dad is well-adjusted, if he loves and encourages his daughter, she comes to appreciate and like herself as a female. By the time she is ushered into adulthood, she will have accumulated a host of wholesome conceptions about herself and her femaleness. She'll feel glad about being a woman; and she'll feel equally good about men being males.

Of course, if Mom is not happy about her own

sex, or if she has rather severe personality problems, the daughter will probably have difficulty appreciating her own sexuality. As she grows up, she will likely send out signals that indicate her own dissatisfaction with being a woman. These feelings may range from mild to severe.

It is important to note that the attitudes of a child toward his or her own sexuality have to do with much more than just their physical makeup and their attitudes toward their bodies. These are crucial elements, but they aren't the only ones. Just by living every day and observing his parents, a child gets a global subconscious picture of how Dad feels about being a male and how Mom feels about being a female. Moment by moment, day by day, a child's perceptions are formed. They can be wholesome, or they can be twisted.

For example, John's mother was an aggressive, rather dominant Christian woman who made most of the decisions in the home. His father was quiet and passive. Later, while attending college, John's problem of ambivalence about himself began to show up. In some ways he felt comfortable being a boy. In other ways he didn't. This plus some experiences outside the home caused an exaggerated interest in sex.

What is at the root of John's problem? The answer is that his earlier family experiences affected his psychosexual development so that there was some questioning, some ambivalence, some confusion about his sexuality as well as the sexuality of females. He also gained satisfaction from hearing and reading about sex. But since he was a devoted Christian, he tried to put a lid on his feelings and desires.

We need to be sensitive to our children's need for sexual identity. Children should be naturally encouraged to feel happy about their sex roles—without the disapproval or regret of the parents. One boy, whose parents had wanted a girl, was given a feminine-sounding name. Since there were already two older brothers, they cast the third one into a girl's role. He learned early that if he were to please his parents, he would have to assume the part of a girl. This was the beginning of a long history that finally led to sex confusion.

It is hard for a girl to accept her own sex if her parents continue to wish she were a boy. She finds it difficult to be herself. This is also true of boys who are handed a girl's part. All too often they are overprotected, overdressed and pampered. Girls who live in such an environment are pressured into such things as male interests or masculine dress and hairstyles.

Children need good models. This means we must spend sufficient time with our children to rub off on them. Only as we play and work together can they gradually gain a healthy image of what it is like to be a man or a woman. Growing children also need to associate with others besides their parents. They need to be with both peers and adults who are comfortable with their own sexual identity and whose daily lives are marked by poise and godliness. Youngsters who associate almost exclusively with one sex are usually at a disadvantage in knowing how the other thinks and feels and reacts.

Our children also need to be helped to see themselves as worthy people with special abilities and interests. Some parents are determined to make their sons into "real he-men" and their girls "real ladies." They maintain such rigid stereotypes they cannot allow their children to develop a breadth of interests. They say things like: "Boys don't play with those things," "That isn't a girl's game," "Don't be a sissy, boys don't cry," or "That's too hard for a girl to do." In attempting to help their sons grow up to be men, their daughters to be women, they are actually doing just the opposite. They are programming their children to force themselves into an unnatural and exaggerated view of masculinity and femininity. The truth is that men should at times cry. And women can participate in many of the same sports that men enjoy.

Abnormal psychosexual development can be prevented. Following the Biblical pattern for families is important: The father is to be a loving, godly leader, but neither a passive nor dominating figure. And the mother is to be a confident Christian lady who finds real fulfillment in her role as wife and mother, and in whatever work God calls her to do.

Psychosexual development goes hand in hand

with total emotional development. Sex can never be separated from personality factors. *Perhaps most sex problems are not really sex problems. Instead, many are reflections of personality problems.* For example, a man who was in full-time Christian service came to a licensed Christian psychologist for therapy. This client had an obsession with pornography. He often sneaked in lewd magazines and read them privately. Being in the Christian ministry, he felt guilty. In fact, he often preached against such things as pornography, smut, dirty books, bad music and prostitution. It was actually a defense against his own problem. Speakers sometimes do this. They preach vigorously against something which is a problem in their own walk with the Lord. A little of this is understandable, and not all bad. We read passages of Scripture or preach sermons which will help to strengthen us against sin. But when we do it consistently, we may be using our preaching as a defense and not as a solution. The man mentioned above never really dealt with his problem, and finally his sin came to light through a prostitute whom he was seeing.

When he started having professional counseling, the therapist could see a definite but complex pattern. In childhood and during the teen years he received no wholesome instruction about sex. His curiosity and the lack of parental guidance turned him in the direction of sex garbage. This in itself brought about much emotional and sex confusion. It also set the stage for later sex problems.

He was gifted, energetic and dynamic, with strong sex drives. As a teenager he experimented with various types of sex activities. At the same time he toyed with religion.

In his family several severe dynamics were taking place. His father, far from an ideal parent, had his own personality and sex problems, and didn't relate well to his son. So the boy grew up without the male identity which he needed.

His mother was a believer, but dominant and manipulative. In her attempts to get him to become more spiritual, she used "spiritual language" and threats. The boy's major identification was with his mother, although he had ambivalent feelings toward her. He loved her, but he also had strong feelings against her. When he found refuge in her, it was at the expense of manipulation and forced, superficial spirituality.

This, too, was to play a significant role in the development of an obsession with pornography later on. Pornography is often used by a man for dominance and conquest over the less powerful—mostly women. It is also used as a weapon of violence, and it provides sexual stimulation.

As an adult and a public figure, his clandestine visits to the prostitute provided an outlet for his hidden anger toward women. It also provided him with a sense of power and significance which he never received from his parents. His prostitute visits also provided fantasies which expanded, distorted and exaggerated reality.

Interestingly, in his rendezvous with the prostitute he did not engage in sexual intercourse. Deep down he felt God would not tolerate it, and that God might strip his "ministry" away from him. Like his childhood experiences, his adult sinful living and his religion were compartmentalized.

As is often common, pornographic experiences may be stored in one's memory and later recalled when engaged in sexual acts. In fact, he recalled these pornographic fantasies when he had intimate relations with his own wife.

When this man first went for professional counseling, he did so against his will. But circumstances forced him to do so. As therapy progressed through the months, he came to understand and reason through the numerous threads which were unknown to him, but which were woven together and which caused him to have a strong obsession with pornography. As he and the Christian psychologist began to apply God's Word to his confused and sordid life, the Bible took on new meaning and eventually brought about healing. Little by little his therapist helped him to resolve numerous feelings and attitudes which had never been resolved in his earlier years. His strong preaching against sin had kept submerging his true feelings, and prevented him from dealing with his problems. In time he became relatively free from the obsession.

In summary, a person's psychosexual development during the growing-up years is significant, with lifetime consequences. Well-adjusted parents who love the Lord can help to prevent a lifetime of confusion and tragedy.

9
Losing Out
Spiritually

We are bombarded
by many powerful persuaders:
worldly television, non-Christian music,
secular radio, and lewd literature
are just a few.

Blessed is the man
who walks not in the counsel of the ungodly,
nor stands in the path of sinners,
nor sits in the seat of the scornful.
But his delight is in the law of the Lord,
and in His law he meditates
day and night.
Psalm 1:1, 2

When a person trusts in Christ as his personal Savior, God's Holy Spirit takes up His abode within that person. From that point on he never walks alone. He not only has God with him, God actually lives within him. "You are partakers of the divine nature" (2 Peter 1:4).

But a person only needs to be saved a short time when he begins to realize that he is actually in a warfare. The archenemy, of course, is Satan: "Be sober, be vigilant; because your adversary the devil walks about like a roaring lion, seeking whom he may devour" (1 Peter 5:8).

Satan tempts the believer in many ways. In fact, he has a whole arsenal of deadly, deceitful devices. Thus, we are told to put on the whole armor of God to protect ourselves: "Put on the whole armor of God, that you may be able to stand against the wiles of the devil" (Ephesians 6:11).

Satan doesn't have special respect for pastors, evangelists, missionaries, Bible teachers or other Christian leaders. In fact, he often concentrates on them because he knows if he can seduce a leader he may also influence thousands of others by his diabolical plan. Satan keeps busy preventing people from trusting the Lord. But if they do embrace Jesus Christ, he makes every attempt to keep them from growing and developing. If he is not successful at that, he then spends years in an effort to cause the Christian to fall and enter into sin.

I believe that Satan often tempts us in an area where we seem to be most vulnerable. Of course, this is different with each person. If we have serious hang-ups such as hostility, insecurity, pride, jealousy, or other undesirable traits, he may zero in on these weak areas. Galatians 5:16, 17 says, "I say then, Walk in the Spirit, and you shall not fulfill the lust of the flesh. For the flesh lusts against the Spirit, and the Spirit against the flesh; and these are contrary to one another, so that you do not do the things that you wish."

Perhaps one of the most difficult things for a Christian leader to do is to continually yield hour by hour to God's Holy Spirit. We get busy "serving the

Lord" and doing so many things that we do not take time to commune with God. We are not keeping the communication lines open with God as He asks us to do: "Pray without ceasing" (1 Thessalonians 5:17).

Another point at which we may succumb is failing to read and obey God's Word. To keep from sinning, the Bible says, "Your Word have I hid in my heart that I might not sin against you" (Psalm 119:11). Again, God admonishes us, "Watch and pray, lest you enter into temptation" (Mark 14:38).

Sometimes we let Satan creep into our lives through the people with whom we associate. God speaks plainly to us about this in Psalm 1:1, 2:

> Blessed is the man who walks not in the counsel of the ungodly, nor stands in the path of sinners, nor sits in the seat of the scornful. But his delight is in the law of the Lord, and in His law he meditates day and night.

Probably few things influence a person as much as another person. We tend to live at the level of the people with whom we associate. Some years ago a Christian man rang my doorbell late on a Sunday night. He wanted to talk about his marriage, which was breaking up. Near the end of our session I asked him if he could put his finger on one or two things that had caused this serious rupture in his family. He looked at me for a moment, then said, "My wife and I have associated with the wrong people. Because we are both well-educated and rather prominent, we enjoyed spending time with the elite. We liked the 'in crowd.' I'm afraid we preferred the sophisticated rather than the saved. Most of our house guests were less spiritual than we, and little by little without realizing it I guess we slid down to their low level."

There are many powerful persuaders in today's society: worldly television, non-Christian music, secular radio, and lewd literature are just a few. Finally, we are spiritually weak and to the point that we become easy prey for Satan. "But every man is tempted when he is drawn away of his own lust, and enticed (James 1:14).

Even churches can play a part in our downfall. The church which is not preaching the gospel or is diluting the gospel message can cause us to cool off and become an easy target for the Devil. One of my first encounters with such a church was in a large city when I was a young man just out of college. I was walking down the street one Sunday morning, and I saw a large, rather imposing church building, went in, and inquired about a young people's Sunday school class. I joined the group, and near the end of the lesson the teacher asked if there was any discussion. At that point I stood and gave a brief testimony. This liberal Sunday school teacher was annoyed by my spiritual remarks and the Scripture verses I quoted. So as I sat down, he said, "Thank you, son, but you'll learn differently as you grow older and become more mature." *He was down on what he was not up on!*

Indeed, there are many religious organizations and churches, but some of them can lead us away from the Lord rather than guiding us to a closer walk with Christ. It is imperative that the Christian leader do all he can to maximize a fresh, simple relationship with the One who died for him. If he doesn't, he is vulnerable to Satan's attacks and finally to a serious fall. Thousands could attest to this truth!

10
What We
Can Do

Rehabilitation is usually
long and costly in pain, grief,
disillusionment, and disappointment.
How much better it is to help people
grow up healthy and to get professional
Christian help rather than see a
beautiful vase crash, then begin
picking up the pieces and trying
to put it back together again.

Therefore as we have opportunity,
let us do good to all,
especially to those who are of the
household of faith.
Galatians 6:10

Wen you hear that a Christian leader has committed gross sins you may ask yourself, "What can I do?" or "How should I feel?" One of the first reactions of a born-again believer is deep disappointment. Whether the transgressor is your pastor, or your friend, or someone you greatly admire or even someone you do not completely agree with theologically, you wish that it had never happened.

As you listen to other people talk about the disaster, you hear many points of view. These various responses can usually be traced back to a person's feelings about himself. If he feels greatly forgiven himself, he will probably have more sympathy for the person. On the other hand, if a person feels basically insecure and has a low self-image, he may even gloat over the problem. He may gain some satisfaction from feeling that another person is worse than he.

Some people, upon hearing that a Christian brother has fallen, feel deeply hurt. For example, a man and his wife shared with me their deep sorrow and pain because their pastor had been caught in a sex problem. "We've trusted him so much," they said. "He even led us to the Lord and later helped us through a difficulty in our own marriage. Now we learn that he has been doing something we're ashamed of. It's going to be difficult to get over this."

To tell this couple they should forget about it would do little good. Their feelings are real to them. Like others, considerable time may be required for them to recover from the tragedy.

When we forgive someone, time and understanding may have to be taken into consideration. We can forgive and yet still feel real pain. Eventually the two will come together.

In some ways the emotions you experience when a trusted Christian leader has fallen are much like those you feel when a friend dies. But there are some differences. In the case of a fallen Christian leader the death never ends. It is a fact that remains. Followers and admirers feel shock, then disbelief, then feelings of self-shame, then anger. A person may want to forget about religion entirely. Another attendant emotion is suspicion. For example, a woman said to me recently, "Every time I look at a pastor or Bible teacher, I wonder if he or she is living in sin."

We may forgive a person, but we must face the fact that there are emotional responses which we can expect people to have for quite a long period. It may even take an especially long time if the leader has often said, "God spoke to me last Thursday" or "God appeared to me and spoke to my spirit." These phrases indicate to the follower that the leader has frequent conversations with God, who is guiding him every hour in a way which the follower has never experienced. So the disappointment is especially great.

A basic factor which you and I should keep in mind when a Christian leader falls into sin is that one of our team members has suffered a severe blow. The emphasis here should be on "team member." The Word of God clearly teaches, "For as we have many members in one body, but all the members do not have the same function, so we being many, are one body in Christ, and individually members of one another" (Romans 12:4, 5). Because of our lack of understanding or our own lack of spiritual maturity or because of our own problems, we may fail to realize that people who have been washed by the blood of Christ and are indwelt by God's Holy Spirit are all on one team. This is true even though a believer may not agree with you and me in every detail. If we keep this fact in mind, it will influence our attitudes toward other members of the Body who have fallen. In other words, one of our troops has been wounded, and it certainly affects all of us.

Something which we must consider as we sort out our feelings and attitudes toward a Christian leader who has fallen is the matter of punishment. When a Christian falls you sometimes hear people say, "Well, he got what was coming to him." In essence, they are saying that the accused deserves punishment and they are going to help bring it about. But this is contrary to the plain teaching of God's Word. The Bible says, "Vengeance is Mine, I will repay, says the Lord" (Romans 12:19).

We don't need to spank each other. Wrong deeds bring with them their own consequences. When we transgress God's law we suffer, and we don't need people to make us suffer more. When we transgress, we not only suffer at the time, but we tend to suffer for the rest of our lives. No one can fully understand the suffering that a person goes through or how long the grief and sorrow remain after a person has committed sin. Indeed, the last thing he needs is fellow-Christians to keep on beating and whipping him.

One day I was talking with a man who had committed immoral acts many years back. He shared the fact that he can never really get away from the incident. "It seems," he said, "that everywhere I go someone has heard about it and brings it up." My heart went out to this man because he has suffered for more than thirty years!

When it comes to sinning, we, as true believers, are all in the same boat. "We have all sinned and come short of the glory of God" (Romans 3:23). For a Christian to point out the sin in a fellow-Christian's life after he's confessed his sin and repented is much like a person who has a disease pointing at another person who has the same illness and saying, "He's sick." There's no justification here for pointing fingers.

When a Christian leader falls, it should cause all of us who are born again to fall on our knees and ask the Lord to help us to be charitable and compassionate. God very plainly says to us, "Brethren, if a man is overtaken in any trespass, you who are spiritual restore such a one in a spirit of gentleness, considering yourself lest you also be tempted" (Galatians 6:1). Our job is to restore, be gentle, and consider ourselves lest we also be tempted.

There are various ways to restore a person, and there are different levels of restoration. For example, you may, in time, forgive a child sex molester, but you wouldn't want him to be around your children. You may forgive a counselor who has taken advantage of you and has committed immoral acts with you. But you wouldn't want to go to him any longer for counseling.

You may have occasional fellowship with a teacher who has molested a college student, but you wouldn't want him back on the faculty.

One of the most important aspects of restoring a person is seeing that he gets professional help so that he can get well. For years I have seen leaders be forgiven by their friends and followers, but they never received the depth of help which they needed. Consequently, they still had their basic tendencies.

Our theme during such a tragic time should be, "Therefore, as we have opportunity, let us do good to all, especially to those who are of the household of faith" (Galatians 6:10).

There are some very practical considerations for us in the prevention of personal moral tragedies. In our own homes we should make sure that as parents we are living godly lives. Also, we should be meeting the basic emotional needs of our children so that they can grow up with healthy feelings and not be so vulnerable to the deceitful cunning of Satan.

In our educational institutions we should be on the lookout for boys and girls who even though they are Christians are not developing in a healthy manner. So many problems could be prevented if we identified them and got help for them early.

It is not enough for teachers to simply impart knowledge to boys and girls. As we teach we should be sensitive to students who seem to be out of step, or who are carrying heavy emotional loads. Each summer, at the Narramore Christian Foundation, we offer a one-week seminar which we call the Teacher Tune-Up. During that time of intensive training we place considerable emphasis on the interpretation of childhood behavior and spotting boys and girls who may be heading for problems a little later on. This type of training should be an important part of the curriculum at all teacher training institutions.

Our Christian colleges and seminaries are ideal places for teachers and administrators to become aware of students who have maladjustments and who are likely to be heading for tragedies later on. As pointed out earlier, serious problems have long root systems. They didn't start yesterday; they started years ago.

A few days ago I met a man in the lobby of a hotel. He quickly identified himself and thanked me for what our organization had done for him.

"I attended," he said, "one of the best Christian colleges in America. But no one knew how I was struggling with feelings of homosexuality. I graduated magna cum laude, then attended one of the finest evangelical seminaries. My struggle with this serious problem continued. I am sure I must have given off little signals continually, but no one ever picked them up, so I never got any help. Finally, as I entered Christian service I went to your clinic in California and had private therapy. In time my problem was completely resolved. Now

I am married, have children, and am tremendously happy. And as you know, I am the head of a national organization which reaches out to help other people."

Thousands of students are walking college and seminary campuses, but need to be noticed and helped before their problems become devastating while in a position of Christian leadership.

Church members and church boards also have an important role in the prevention or solution of tragic moral problems. They should be alert to their pastor and to other church staff members who can benefit from professional training. Let me explain. The Narramore Christian Foundation, for example, has provided short-term, professional training for more than 4,000 ministers and missionaries and their spouses. These remarkably fine Christian leaders have come to our campus in Rosemead for a two-week seminar. They lived on campus and were given psychological tests, group counseling, individual counseling, and training by a large staff of godly psychologists, medical doctors and other specialists. The results have been excellent.

As we look back over the years and consider these 4,000 or more, we realize several things.

After taking several psychological tests and identifying areas in their lives that deserved attention, they were eager to improve. They did not come especially because they had problems. They came because they wanted to improve the quality of their life and to be more effective servants of Christ. However, we have been impressed by the number who have thanked us for enriching or even saving their marriage and their ministry.

Medical doctors and other professionals get the finest training they can before they enter into professional practice. But that's just the beginning. Once or twice a year they usually attend seminars and receive further training so that they can render the best service possible to their people.

In contrast, I have seen pastors, evangelists and other Christian leaders minister to others for years and never go for in-service professional training themselves. This is a tragedy; it's tragic not only for the pastor but also for his people.

Rehabilitation is usually long and costly: costly in money, pain, grief, disillusionment, and disappointment. How much better it is to encourage a Christian leader to get professional Christian training rather than to stand by and see a beautiful vase crash, then begin picking up the pieces and trying to put it back together again.

In summary, we evangelical Christians have the most wonderful possession in all the world—eternal life through Christ. But some of our people, including some leaders, have severe problems which finally come to light through devastating immoral experiences.

We can all be healthy—both spiritually and emotionally. But if we do not take the steps to achieve this well-being, hundreds and even thousands more of our leaders will experience tragic falls and sex involvements in the future!

About
the Author

Dr. Clyde M. Narramore is often referred to as the dean of Christian psychologists. Perhaps more than any other man, he has been responsible for the Christian psychology movement in America.

Dr. Narramore received his doctorate from Columbia University, New York City, and is a licensed psychologist. He is a prolific writer and a frequent speaker in Washington, D.C. at such departments as the State Department, Pentagon, FBI and the CIA. He has also spoken to the President's staff at the White House.

He was the founder and first president of the Rosemead Graduate School of Psychology.

Dr. Narramore is also the founder and president

of the Narramore Christian Foundation, an international ministry specializing in counseling and the training of leaders. The Narramore Christian Foundation is located on a ten-acre campus in Rosemead, California, and offers one-week and two-week seminars for pastors, missionaries, business people, educators, lay counselors, and sons and daughters of missionaries. Seminars are also offered for those interested in vocational planning, as well as for senior groups.

Literature, films, videocassettes and audiocassettes as well as phone referrals are available by writing or phoning Dr. Narramore's office, Box 5000, Rosemead CA 91770; phone 818/288-7000.

Study Questions for Discussion

GROUP LEADER:

Many people gain much more from a book if they have an opportunity to discuss the content with others.

What follows is a short list of questions for each of the ten chapters, and extra space for notemaking or reflections of this book. These may be especially valuable for study groups, classes, fellowships, families, teachers, students, senior citizens, parents, singles, staff, and others.

You may wish to use these questions with such a group, or with special friends. In doing so, it is suggested that you spend sufficient time with each question to enable participants to gain a depth of insight, and to express themselves adequately.

For example, a group of questions relating to one chapter of the book may require thirty minutes to an hour. In fact, some people will not feel free to express themselves until after a point has been discussed at length. Consequently, the ten groups of questions may require five to ten sessions of discussion.

The leader should encourage each member of the group to talk, keeping his own discussion at a minimum in order to draw each person out.

After a person has shared, the group leader may ask him to share further, or to explain in more detail what he means. This will benefit the participant as well as other members of the group.

Chapter 1: Shocked by the News

1. In this chapter the author brings out the fact that when a Christian leader falls and people hear about it they are usually shocked. Why don't most people pick up the clues that a person is maladjusted—as they observe him, hear him, or as they read his books?

2. What are some clues that you and I can notice in other people which tell us that a person may have some "inside" problems?

3. The roots of people's problems usually go back many years. Let's discuss this. Why is this usually true?

4. Why might many news reporters seem to gain a measure of satisfaction from reporting on the fact that a Christian leader has fallen? What would cause them to feel this way?

Chapter 2: Rank and Its Privileges

1. Why do some people, including Christians, take advantage of their rank (their leadership role) and abuse it by exercising various privileges?

2. Undoubtedly some parents take advantage of their size, strength, intelligence and experience when dealing with their sons and daughters. How might a parent take advantage of his parental rank, and why would he or she do this?

3. How should you and I, in our daily living, guard against taking advantage of the status and rank which we have at the office, in the community, at home, at church and elsewhere?

Chapter 3: Public Vulnerability

1. In this chapter Dr. Narramore points out that as we have more and more contacts with people and are in the public eye, we become more vulnerable, especially in romantic and intimate circumstances. What are some of the ways in which any Christian may become vulnerable in these situations?

2. How can you and I avoid unwholesome and sinful entanglements in our day-to-day contacts?

3. How might a pastor or any other Christian leader guard against intimate entanglements in his service to the public?

Chapter 4: Pride Goeth Before

1. Some people are perhaps more likely to become prideful than others. Why may this be true?

2. What are some of the evidences that a person is prideful?

3. Can a person be truly humble and still have a healthy self-image?

4. Why might a person think that another is prideful when actually he is not?

Chapter 5: What's at Home?

1. In this chapter the author makes this statement: "A man usually brings his wife and family to work with him." What is meant by this—and how does it show itself in a man's or woman's conduct on the job?

2. When spouses are treated considerably worse at home than at the office, how are they likely to feel and what are they likely to do?

3. What are some of the basic causes of maladjustment for a husband or a wife? What might their problems stem from?

4. When a church interviews a minister with the possibility of calling him as their pastor, what can the pulpit committee do to make certain that the prospective new pastor has an excellent relationship with his wife?

Chapter 6: Emotional Adjustment

1. In this chapter Dr. Narramore notes several basic emotional needs which cry out for fulfillment throughout childhood. Among them are a) feeling and being told you are loved, b) knowing you are worthwhile, c) feeling that you belong, d) being relatively free from fear, e) feeling relatively free from guilt. Take one of these and show how it was met quite well throughout your childhood. Then take one and explain how it was *not* met very well when you were growing up. If possible let's all share in this.

2. Will you now connect some current adult behavior of yours to the fact that one of these basic emotional needs was well met in your childhood? Also choose one emotional need that was *not* met well when you were growing up and show how it is affecting you today.

3. A licensed psychologist gives personality inventories and psychological tests which indicate the extent of a person's emotional adjustment in a number of areas. How might this type of professional service be used?

Chapter 7: Pre-salvation Experiences

1. Why might the experiences a person has before he is saved continue to have an impact upon him long after he has trusted Christ as his personal Savior?

2. Proverbs 22:6 says, "Train up a child in the way he should go, and when he is old he will not depart from it." What can we expect to happen if a child is raised in the way he should *not* go? How might these negative factors affect a person even after he has been saved?

3. Let's discuss the importance of being saved at an early age and living a consistent life for Christ.

Chapter 8: Psychosexual Development

1. Dr. Narramore states that the term *psychosexual* has to do with the mental and emotional attitudes which a person holds toward himself as a sexual being and toward other people as sexual beings. What are some of the dynamics and conditions in a family that would cause a child to grow up with good healthy feelings about his own sex, as well as the sex of the opposite gender?

2. Why is it important for a child to have good sex role models in both the mother and the father?

3. If a child has grown up without good sex role models and with unwholesome experiences either in or outside the family, what can he do as an adult to counteract these negative influences and personality shapers?

4. Why might a person preach and teach strongly against sin, yet at the same time be committing those sins himself?

Chapter 9: Losing Out Spiritually

1. What influences (or effects) should the Holy Spirit have upon the behavior of a person who has been born again?

2. What are some of the factors that would cause a person to lose out spiritually and to enter into sinful acts?

3. The author points out in this chapter that a person who has personality problems may become an easy target for many evil things and sinful people. Why is this?

4. How could a church possibly cause a person to become less spiritual and less Biblically minded?

Chapter 10: What We Can Do

1. In this last chapter Dr. Narramore indicates that a transgressor goes through several stages after his sin has found him out. Followers of Christian leaders may also go through several stages after they have learned that their leader has engaged in immoral acts. What are some of these stages?

2. What might each of the following do to prevent a person from becoming an adult who engages in immorality: a) the home, b) the school, c) the Christian college and seminary, d) the church?

3. As you reflect upon this book, please share one or two things that have been most helpful to you.